A SOLDIER'S LIFE IN
ANCIENT EGYPT

A SOLDIER'S LIFE IN
ANCIENT EGYPT

Fiona Corbridge

W
FRANKLIN WATTS
LONDON • SYDNEY

Illustrations by:
Mark Bergin
Giovanni Caselli
Chris Molan
Lee Montgomery
Peter Visscher
Maps by Stefan Chabluk

First published in 2006 by
Franklin Watts
338 Euston Road
London NW1 3BH

Franklin Watts Australia
Hachette Children's Books
Level 17/207 Kent Street
Sydney NSW 2000

Series editor: John C. Miles
Art director: Jonathan Hair

The text of this book is based on *Going to
War in Ancient Egypt* by Dr Anne Millard
© Franklin Watts 2000. It is produced for
Franklin Watts by Painted Fish Ltd.
Designer: Rita Storey

A CIP catalogue record
for this book is available
from the British Library

ISBN 0 7496 6490 8
Dewey classification: 355.00932

Printed in China

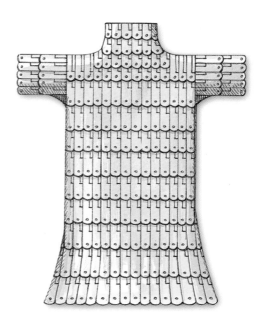

CONTENTS

Ancient Egypt
- *The ancient Egyptians had a system of picture writing called hieroglyphics.*

- *The people were skilled craftworkers.*

- *The ancient Egyptians built huge monuments to their dead kings, made out of mud bricks.*

Kings and pharaohs
- *The rulers of Egypt were called "king". This was short for "king of Upper and Lower Egypt".*

- *In later times (during the New Kingdom), the rulers were known as "pharaoh".*

Gold and amethyst make-up jar

THE ANCIENT EGYPTIANS

The ancient Egyptians lived in Egypt thousands of years ago. Slowly, two kingdoms grew: Upper Egypt (in the south) and Lower Egypt (in the north).

To protect their land, the Egyptians built up an army to fight off attackers. They also used the army to conquer peoples who lived nearby and their land.

Jewel worn by an Egyptian princess

Ancient Egypt
c. 5000–30 BCE

The long history of ancient Egypt is divided into different time periods and kingdoms (see the whole list on page 7).

Old Kingdom
c. 2700–2100 BCE

The ancient Egyptians became very good at art, literature and science. Kings were buried in huge stone pyramids.

Middle Kingdom
c. 2040–1790 BCE

Egypt conquered the neighbouring country of Nubia. The army built huge fortresses on Egypt's southern and eastern frontiers.

HITTITES

MITTANI

CYPRUS

Byblos ○ ● Kadesh
Megiddo ● CANAAN
Joppa ○ ● Jericho

MEDITERRANEAN SEA

LOWER EGYPT

Alexandria ○
LIBYA   Buto ● ○ Avaris
Siwa Oasis   Memphis ●
             SINAI
Bahriya Oasis ○ Fayum
             Herakleopolis ●

Farafra Oasis

            UPPER
            EGYPT   Abydos ●
Dakla   RED SEA
Oasis   Thebes/Luxor ●
                   Hierankopolis ●
Kharga Oasis   ○ Aswan

                   NUBIA
                   Buhen

                   Semnah

                   KUSH

            Gebel Barkal ○

The history of ancient Egypt

Predynastic Egypt
c. 5000 BCE

Archaic Egypt
c. 3100 BCE

Old Kingdom
c. 2700–2100 BCE

First Intermediate Period
c. 2100–2040 BCE

Middle Kingdom
c. 2040–1790 BCE

Second Intermediate Period
c. 1790–1550 BCE

New Kingdom
c. 1550–1080 BCE

Third Intermediate Period
c. 1080–664 BCE

Late Period
664–332 BCE

Ptolemaic Egypt
332–30 BCE

▮ The Egyptian empire

🏰 Major forts

New Kingdom
c. 1550–1080 BCE

Hyksos invaders were driven out of Egypt. Egypt became rich and successful. Kings were buried in the Valley of the Kings at Thebes.

The lighthouse at Alexandria, c. 330 BCE

Ptolemaic Egypt
332–30 BCE

Alexander the Great drove out the Persians. One of his generals, Ptolemy, became king of Egypt. In 31 BCE, the Romans made Egypt part of the Roman Empire.

EGYPT'S FIRST ARMIES

During the time of the Old Kingdom (c. 2700–2100 BCE) the kings of Egypt had a small army. In the Middle Kingdom (c. 2040–1790 BCE) the kings began to build an empire by taking over other lands. This made Egypt bigger and more powerful. They had a large army and used it to conquer the neighbouring country of Nubia.

Nubian mercenary

Egyptian warrior (soldier) of the Middle Kingdom

Leather straps (for protection)

Leather-covered wooden shield

MERCENARIES

To make their army bigger, kings used mercenaries (soldiers who could be hired to fight for the army of another people or country).

From around 2000 BCE onwards, the kings of Egypt paid Nubians to fight for them. The Nubians were very good archers.

The first Egyptian soldiers sometimes wore animal tails to make them look fierce

Wrestling matches helped soldiers to keep fit

KINGS AT WAR

In Predynastic times, kings led their troops into battle. In the Old Kingdom, kings did not fight. In the Middle Kingdom, kings became warriors again.

PRIVATE ARMIES

In the Old and Middle Kingdom, Egypt was divided into 42 nomes (districts). These had private armies for the king to use when he needed them.

During the First Intermediate Period (c. 2100–2040 BCE), the nomes used their armies to fight each other. They even fought against the king himself.

EGYPT'S ENEMIES

Canaanite warrior

Libyans

The Libyans lived in the desert. They tried to invade Egypt because it had good land for farming. Egyptian kings usually fought off their attacks, but in the First Intermediate Period the Libyans managed to grab land to live in.

Libyan warrior

Kushite warrior

Bedouin and Canaanites

The Bedouin people lived in the desert. They often attacked Egyptian traders. Canaanites came from Canaan. Some traded with Egypt, but others attacked it.

Nubians and Kushites

Nubians came from the south. The Egyptians traded with them and later ruled them. The Kushites lived further south. The Egyptians only managed to conquer them in the New Kingdom (c. 1550–1080 BCE).

ENEMIES OF EGYPT

The armies of ancient Egypt had to deal with rivals, rebels and invaders.
In the Second Intermediate Period (c. 1790–1550 BCE), the Egyptians had to fight off an invasion by the Hyksos people. This made them more warlike, and the army became bigger and better trained. The Egyptians then went on to conquer other peoples to make a big empire.

Hittite warrior

Syrian archer

Sherden warrior

MITANNI AND HITTITES
Egypt's first great rivals were the Mitanni. Then the Hittites crushed the Mitanni and became Egypt's most dangerous enemies.

SEA PEOPLES
The Sea Peoples probably came from Greece and Turkey. They included the Sherden and Peleset peoples. They started raiding Egypt around 1500 BCE. Some were captured and joined the king's bodyguard.

CANAANITES AND SYRIANS
Egypt conquered Canaan and Syria. But the people hated being ruled by the Egyptians and often rebelled (fought them). They got help from the Mitanni and Hittites, who were great enemies of the Egyptians.

CHARIOTS

The Hyksos managed to invade Egypt easily because they had chariots (two-wheeled carts pulled by horses). The Egyptians had not seen these before, but quickly decided to build their own.

Egyptian commanders had to change their battle tactics for the new chariots, and work out the best way to protect their soldiers from the chariots of the enemy. Charioteers and chariot soldiers had special training. The infantry (foot soldiers) who fought alongside the chariots also needed to be trained.

An Egyptian prince drives a chariot and horses at a gallop

Tactics
Tactics are special plans that an army makes to try and win in battle.

Chariot crews
Chariots had a two-man crew: the charioteer (driver) and a chariot soldier.

FAST TRAVEL

Until chariots arrived, the fastest way to travel was to run. The speed of a chariot must have seemed terrifying.

Horses and chariots were expensive, and rich people bought them to show off their wealth.

Soldiers who fought the enemy from chariots in the battlefield needed a lot of skill, especially when the horses galloped. The chariots were made of wood and were very light. They could move fast and turn easily.

FORTRESSES

The Egyptians knew that they needed to guard their frontiers and trade routes. In the Middle Kingdom, around 2000 BCE, they built two lines of fortresses on the southern and eastern frontiers of Egypt.

During the New Kingdom (c. 1550–1080 BCE) the Egyptians built forts on the north-west frontier.

Frontier
The edge of a country's territory or land.

Trade routes
The route used by traders (land or sea) to take goods to sell in other lands.

Fortress
A group of buildings protected by thick walls. A fort is like a fortress, but smaller.

The governor inspects the defences

Prisoners

🔱 BUILDING AND DESIGN

The walls of a fortress were very strong – they could be 10 metres high and 5 metres thick. Many forts had an inner area like a fortified town, and an outer area which was also heavily fortified. This was surrounded by a deep ditch. Some forts were near a river and used ships to fetch supplies.

The fort at Buhen had arrow slits for archers to shoot enemies coming from any direction.

LIFE IN A FORTRESS

Soldiers were busy even when they were not at war. They went out on patrol, looking for signs of trouble, and guarded traders. They also kept an eye on conquered peoples and anyone coming into Egypt.

The huge fortress at Semnah, built during the Middle Kingdom

TRIBUTE

Conquered peoples had to regularly give their conquerors goods, crops or precious items such as gold. This was called "tribute".

During the New Kingdom, Egypt's kings became extremely rich from tributes paid by the peoples in their empire.

This tomb painting shows Syrians bringing tributes

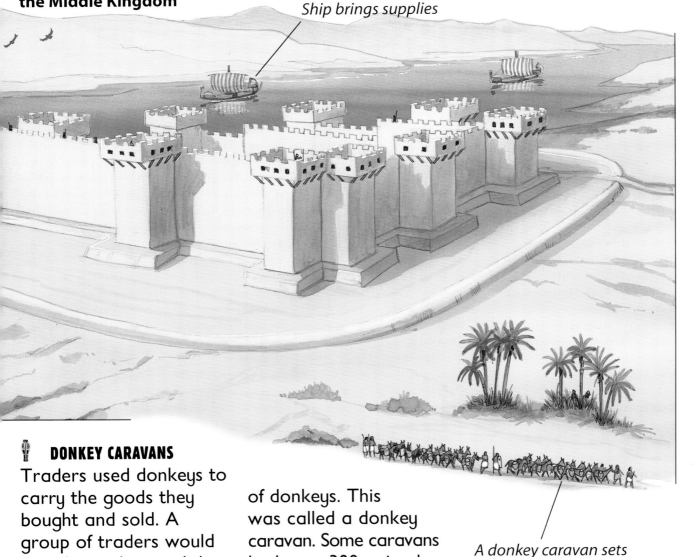

Ship brings supplies

A donkey caravan sets off on an expedition

DONKEY CARAVANS

Traders used donkeys to carry the goods they bought and sold. A group of traders would travel together, with lots of donkeys. This was called a donkey caravan. Some caravans had over 300 animals.

SIEGE!

If the Egyptians did not defeat an enemy in battle, they might attack an enemy fortress or walled city. They surrounded it and cut off supplies of food and water. This was called a siege. It was a good way to force the people inside to surrender (give up).

STARTING A SIEGE
Troops surrounded the city to cut off supplies. Then scouts kept watch for any soldiers coming to help the city.

LADDERS
The Egyptians used ladders to climb the city's walls. Some of the ladders had wheels so that they could be pushed up to the walls more easily.

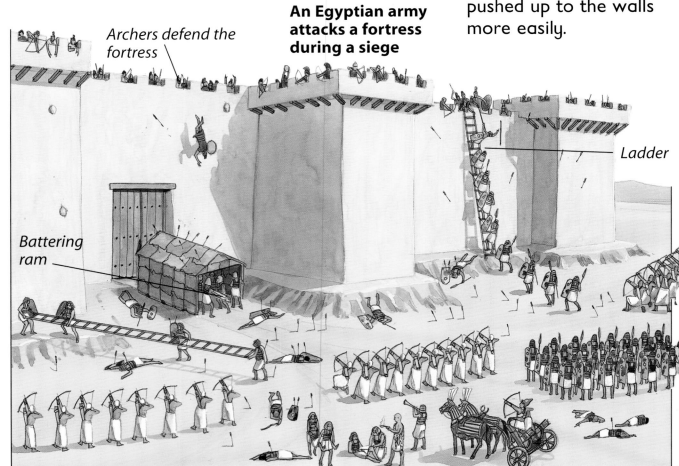

Archers defend the fortress

An Egyptian army attacks a fortress during a siege

Ladder

Battering ram

TUTHMOSIS III
Tuthmosis III was a great warrior king. He led a siege of the city of Joppa in Canaan and smuggled 200 Egyptian soldiers into the city by hiding them in baskets that were supposed to hold presents for the enemy queen. The Egyptian soldiers climbed out and opened the city gates to let in the rest of the Egyptian army.

VICTORY

Capture
Ordinary prisoners of war became slaves and were made to work for the Egyptians.

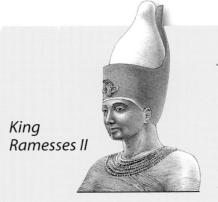

King Ramesses II

Execution
After a siege, defeated enemy leaders were executed (killed).

Keeping a record
All kings wrote about their victories, but never their defeats. The battle of Kadesh was a draw, but Ramesses II managed to make it sound like a great victory.

BATTERING RAMS
Troops used a battering ram to break down city gates. This was a tree trunk with a point at one end. The men using the ram were protected from arrows by a roof.

SLAVES
Some prisoners became household slaves. They were usually well treated, especially if they had skills. Slaves had rights and could even own property.

Nubian slave girl dancing

Battering ram

Slaves
Some slaves helped to build temples. Others worked in quarries and mines. Household slaves worked in the home. If they were good at woodwork, spinning, weaving or dancing, the Egyptians were pleased and treated them especially well.

TRAINING

Most soldiers volunteered to join the army. The king also kept a list of young men who he called up in turn to serve in the army for a time. They were called conscripts.

New recruits had to practise marching and learn to use weapons. Then they were ready to join an army unit.

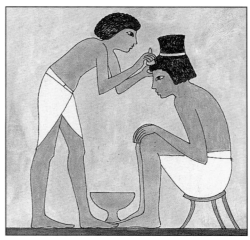

HAIRCUT
New recruits to the army had to have a haircut.

Marching order of the army

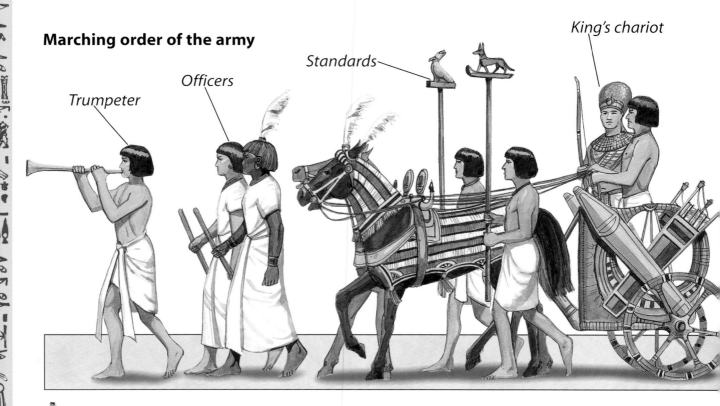

Trumpeter

Officers

Standards

King's chariot

WEAPONS AND CHARIOTS
Recruits were trained to use many weapons, but became experts with one or two. They joined the army unit that used these weapons.

Each army division had 500 chariots. A chariot was pulled by two horses. It held a charioteer (driver) and a soldier. A mass of charging chariots was terrifying for the enemy.

An Egyptian prince learns how to fire a bow

OFFICERS

Officers had a lot of things to learn. They had to be good at using weapons and driving a chariot. They also had to study tactics to help them win battles.

They even learned about the geography of the lands where they were going to work or fight, and the customs of the peoples there.

Mercenaries
There were many Nubian, Libyan and Sherden mercenaries in Egyptian armies until about 1080 BCE.

After that time, Greek mercenaries replaced them.

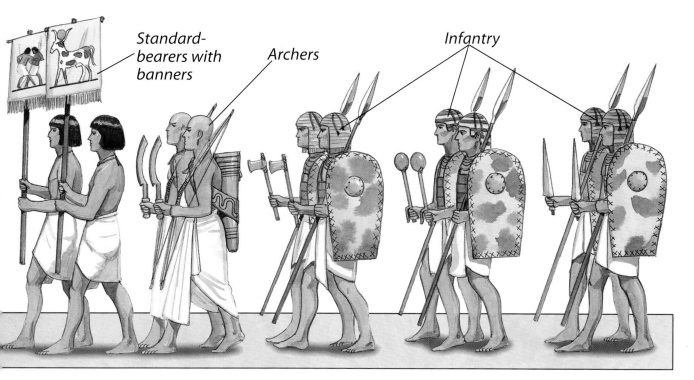

Standard-bearers with banners

Archers

Infantry

STANDARDS AND SIGNALS

Each army unit had its own standard. This was a long pole with the unit's badges or symbols.

It was carried by the standard-bearer. In battle, the standard acted as a meeting point for soldiers.

In battle, commands such as "Charge!" and "Retreat!" were given by a trumpeter blowing notes on a trumpet.

READY FOR BATTLE

By the time of the New Kingdom (c. 1550–1080 BCE) the army was made up of divisions. A division contained 5,000 men (4,000 infantry and 1,000 who fought from chariots).

Each division was divided into companies of 200 men. The men lived together in groups of ten.

Blue war helmet

THE BLUE WAR HELMET

Kings in the New Kingdom led their armies into battle wearing a blue war helmet.

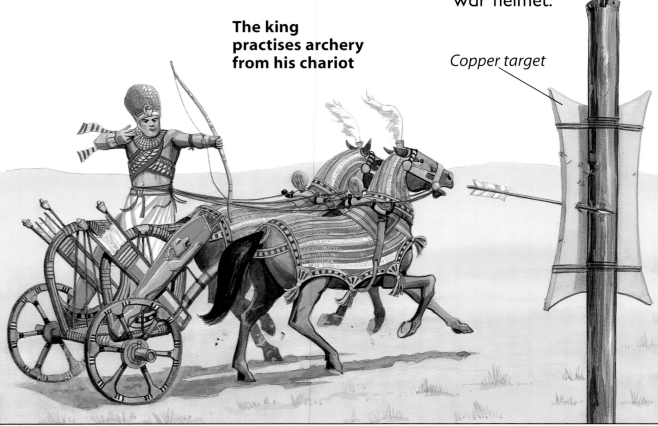

The king practises archery from his chariot

Copper target

CHARIOTS

The Egyptian army had chariots for fighting, not for moving soldiers about. The chariots were light and speedy. The army used them to break up lines of enemy infantry and to help their own infantry. All the charioteers (drivers), chariot soldiers and horses had a lot of training to get them ready for battle.

IN THE ARMY

Daily practice
Every day, soldiers had to practise fighting so that they were ready for battle.

Counting hands
After a battle, soldiers cut off the right hands of dead enemy soldiers and put them in piles. Scribes counted up the hands and wrote down the number for official records.

Wooden carving of a scout

Scouts
The Egyptian army used scouts. They rode horses and went ahead to find out more about the enemy. Scouts could move quickly to report what they had seen. This helped the army to decide on tactics.

ARMY RANKS
The king was the commander-in-chief of the army. A general commanded each division, and officers were in charge of the companies and smaller units.

Doctors, priests, scribes, armourers, messengers, heralds, spies, grooms and servants also worked for the army.

ADVISERS AND SPIES
The king had an army council of advisers to help him. He also had spies who collected information.

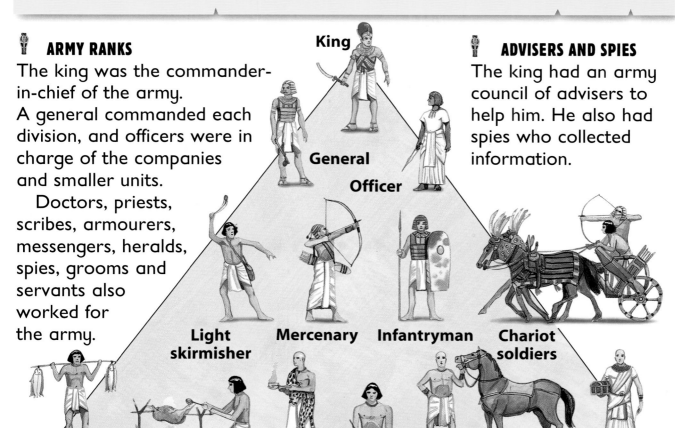

King

General

Officer

Light skirmisher

Mercenary

Infantryman

Chariot soldiers

Servant

Cook

Priest

Scribe

Groom and armourer

Doctor

WEAPONS AND ARMOUR

In the New Kingdom, the infantry had three kinds of soldier.

The Braves went on the most dangerous missions. The Veterans fought in the front ranks (rows) in battle. The Recruits were less experienced soldiers. They made up the second ranks and reserves, fighting behind the Veterans.

ARMOUR

Soldiers wore a cuirass (body armour) made out of padded linen. It was sometimes strengthened with leather bands or scales. They had a padded linen helmet to protect the head and carried a shield.

Protection
By the time of the New Kingdom, soldiers needed good armour because the enemy's weapons were stronger and more dangerous. They also had to be well protected to help them survive chariot charges.

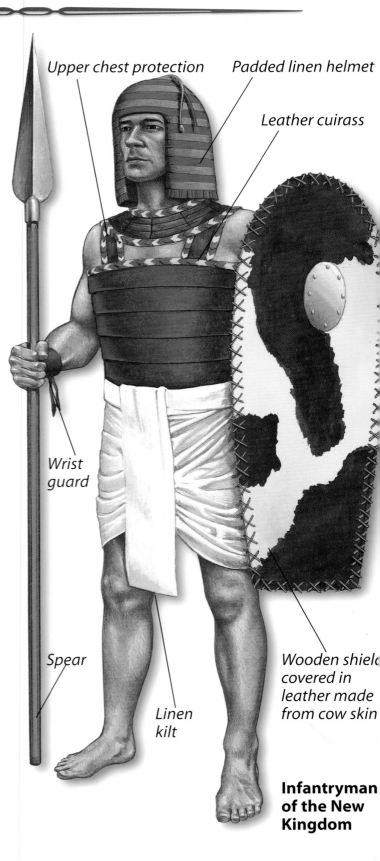

Upper chest protection

Padded linen helmet

Leather cuirass

Wrist guard

Spear

Linen kilt

Wooden shield covered in leather made from cow skin

Infantryman of the New Kingdom

WEAPONS

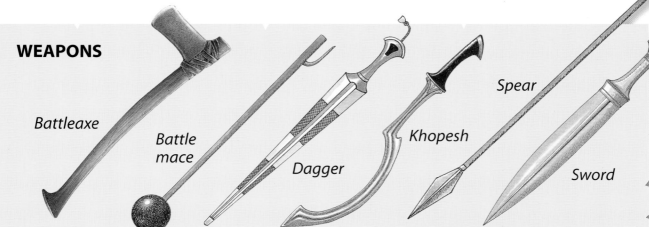

Battleaxe

Battle mace

Dagger

Khopesh

Spear

Sword

Bronze
By the time of the New Kingdom, weapons were made of bronze. These pictures show some of them. Soldiers also had bows and arrows.

Iron
By 1000 BCE, some people in the Middle East knew how to make iron. The Egyptians had to buy iron to make weapons that were as good as theirs.

New weapons
The Hyksos people had two weapons that the Egyptians soon copied. These were a curved sword called a khopesh, and a new kind of bow. This was stronger than an Egyptian bow, so it could fire arrows further.

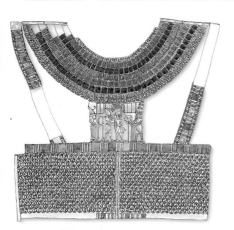

Tutankhamun's ceremonial armour

TOO GOOD FOR BATTLE!
Kings had ceremonial armour to wear on special occasions. Some was found in the tomb of King Tutankhamun. It was made of gold scales and semi-precious stones.

ARCHERS
Archers wore a special brace to protect their wrists when firing a bow and arrow. This was usually made of leather.

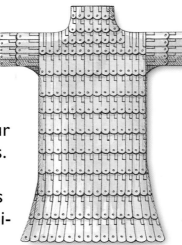

Mail shirt, c. 1200 BCE

Scales from a mail shirt

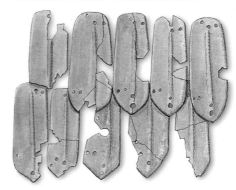

MAIL SHIRTS
A mail shirt was armour made of bronze scales sewn on a padded linen shirt. It was flexible, so the wearer could move easily. It would have been very expensive and perhaps only used by officers and kings.

MAKING CAMP

When they were on a campaign, the soldiers set up a camp every night. Workers piled up a mound of earth around an area big enough for the camp. They pushed shields into the earth to make a protective wall. Inside the wall, troops put up tents in neat rows.

CAMP LIFE

The army travelled with servants and doctors to look after the troops. Grooms and vets took care of the animals, and armourers repaired weapons. Priests looked for signs from the gods that would tell the king what to do.

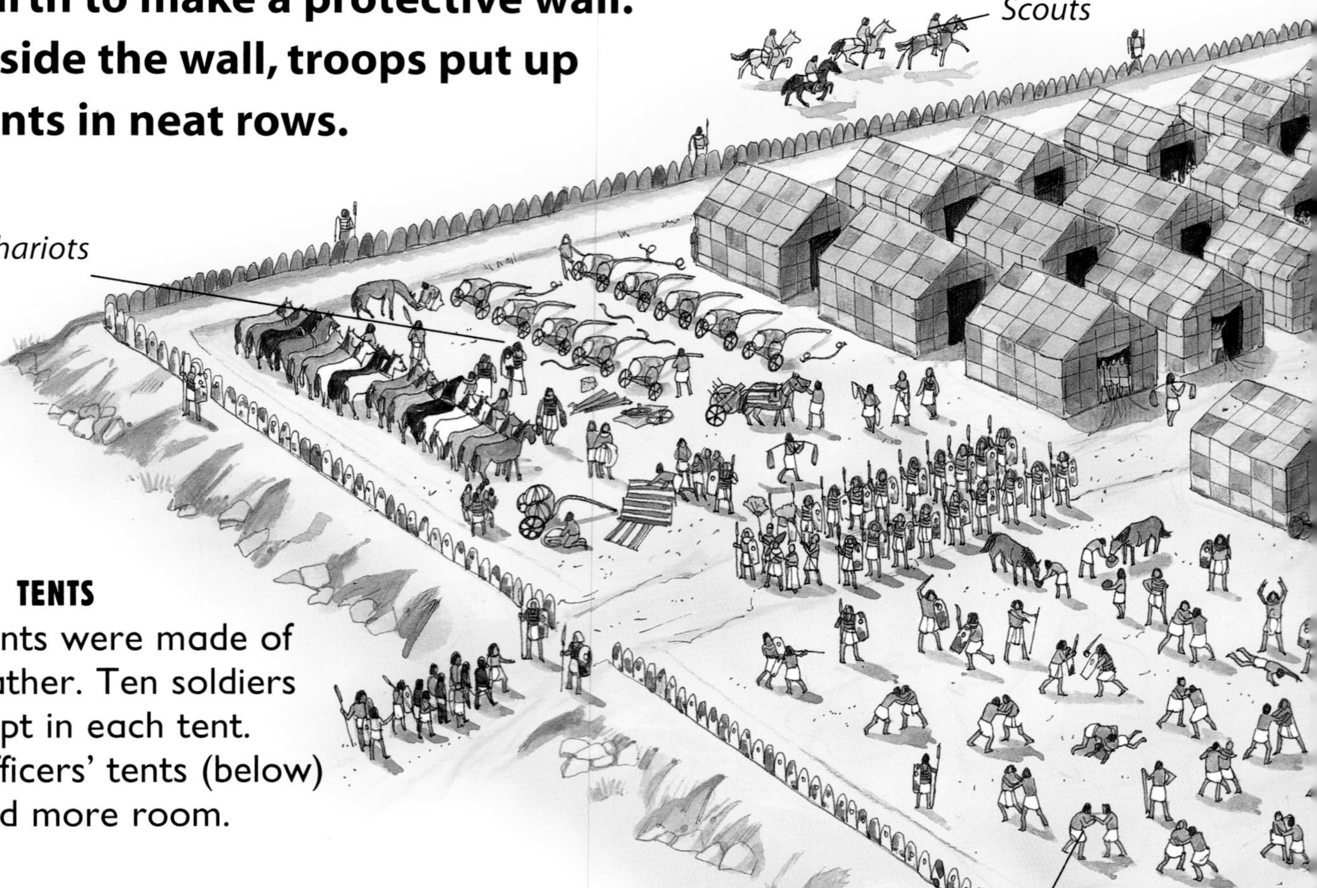

Scouts

Chariots

TENTS

Tents were made of leather. Ten soldiers slept in each tent. Officers' tents (below) had more room.

SCOUTS

Scouts on horses patrolled the area around the camp to make sure that the army was not in danger of a surprise attack.

Troops practise wrestling to keep fit

DIPLOMACY

Diplomacy is a way of staying friendly with other people. It means dealing with them carefully to prevent trouble. Diplomats make sure that their country stays on good terms with others. In ancient Egypt, diplomats lived at foreign courts. Kings and rulers sent each other presents. All this helped to prevent wars.

The gods
The ancient Egyptians believed in many gods. The camp had a special tent where statues of the gods were kept.

The king of the gods was Amen-Re. He was said to tell the king when to go to war.

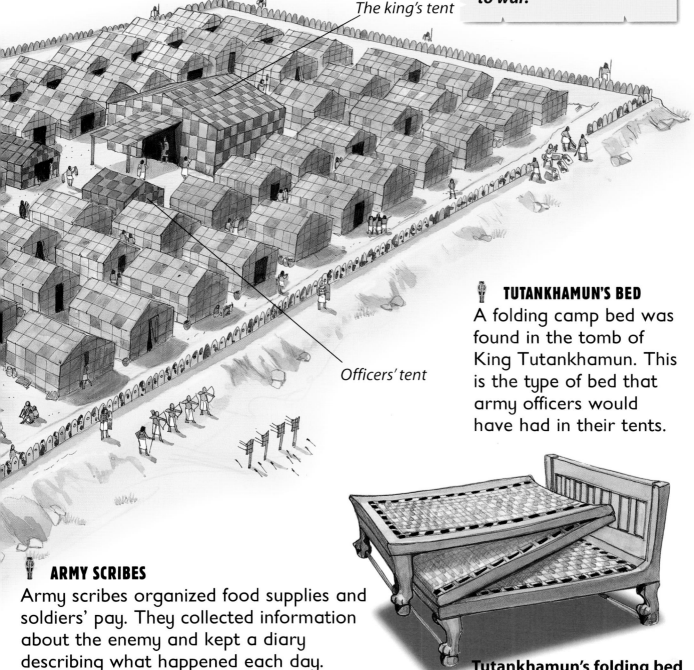

The king's tent

Officers' tent

TUTANKHAMUN'S BED

A folding camp bed was found in the tomb of King Tutankhamun. This is the type of bed that army officers would have had in their tents.

ARMY SCRIBES

Army scribes organized food supplies and soldiers' pay. They collected information about the enemy and kept a diary describing what happened each day.

Tutankhamun's folding bed

GUARDING THE EMPIRE

Soldiers spent time doing different things. They went on campaigns, did garrison duty, or worked in a base.

Garrison duty meant guarding a fortress, fort or base. Soldiers working in the bases lived in huts called barracks. Ten men lived in each hut. Their families often lived nearby.

TRADE

Some trading expeditions needed soldiers to protect them. Tribesmen and thieves sometimes tried to steal the traders' goods. Traders bringing back incense were often attacked. (Incense smells nice and is used in religious ceremonies.)

A trading expedition returns

GUARD DUTY

Some soldiers were sent out on guard duty. Criminals and prisoners worked at mines and quarries. They had to be guarded to stop them escaping. The caravans going to and from the mines also had to be guarded.

Running fortresses and forts
A troop commander was in charge of a fort.
Garrison commanders were in charge of several forts.
Overseers of fortresses were responsible for all the forts on a frontier.

Border guards talk to a Bedouin

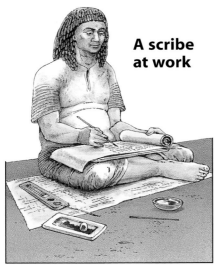

A scribe at work

CHECKING THE FRONTIERS

Bedouin tribespeople often brought their flocks to Egypt to feed on the plants there. Border guards counted how many people came in and made sure that they all left later!

FOR THE RECORD

Army scribes sent the vizier (chief minister) details about everything that happened in the garrison and along the frontiers.

An Egyptian fights a Peleset raider

CITY DEFENDERS

Troops and medjay (police) were stationed in cities. They had to defend the city and fight off raiders, prevent any trouble, guard cemeteries and catch criminals.

SEA BATTLES

Egypt had a strong navy and soldiers were often moved around by ship instead of marching.

The Egyptians fought many sea battles. They won a great victory over the Sea Peoples in 1180 BCE. But they lost the battle of Actium against the Romans in 31 BCE. After this, Egypt became part of the Roman Empire.

SAILORS AND MARINES

Ships had a crew of sailors who rowed the ship and looked after the sail. A captain was in charge.

Ships also carried soldiers called marines, who fought in sea battles. Large ships had up to 200 marines, led by a standard-bearer.

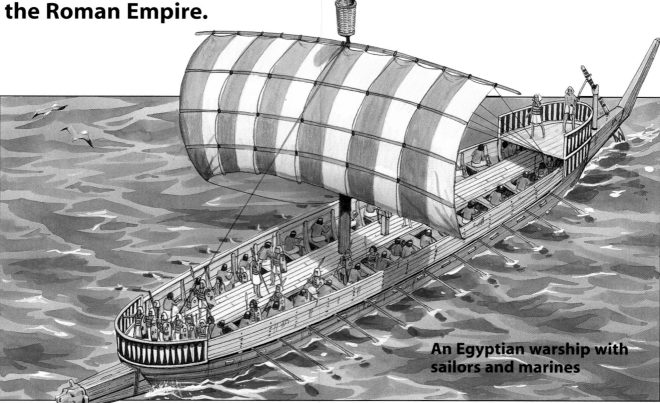

An Egyptian warship with sailors and marines

FIGHTING SHIPS

Ships were made of wooden planks, fixed together with pegs and ropes. This meant that they could be taken apart easily, carried over land or around a waterfall in a river, then quickly put back together.

A ship had rowers on each side who used oars to move the ship along. It also had a sail and a steering oar.

NAVAL WARFARE

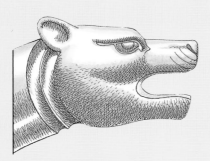

Lion's head
The bronze lion's head fitted to the prow (front) of King Ramesses III's warships was there to try and ram a hole in an enemy ship and sink it.

Battling against raiders
The Sea Peoples were pirates and raiders. They destroyed the Hittite empire and then kept attacking Egypt along its northern coast.

Lookouts
A famous tomb painting shows a ship carrying Nubian mercenaries. The men in this part of the painting seem to be lookouts keeping watch for danger.

The Sea Peoples invaded Egypt during the reign of Ramesses III, c. 1180 BCE

VICTORY FOR EGYPT
In about 1180 BCE, thousands of Sea Peoples set out to find new homes. That meant taking land from someone else. Ramesses III stopped them in two great battles – one on land, and one at sea.

Sea Peoples
Peoples who probably came from Greece, its colonies in Turkey and the Aegean Islands. They left their homelands because of fighting and a lack of food. They destroyed many cities.

REWARDS

Men who joined the army in the New Kingdom had things to look forward to. Soldiers who took part in winning campaigns became heroes. Being a soldier was also a good way of getting rich. Brave fighters were given rewards, and soldiers earned treasure after successful campaigns.

LAND REWARDS
Soldiers who did well in battle were given land when they retired. Many people did not own any land, so this was a valuable reward.

Gold battleaxe given as a reward

GOLD REWARDS
Queen Mother Ahhotep, fighting on behalf of her son, was given three golden flies – the highest award for bravery.

A soldier collects his rewards, including a Nubian slave girl

Queen Ahhotep's golden flies

TREASURE AND SLAVES
When a city was captured, the soldiers got a share of any treasure. They were also given some of the prisoners of war as slaves to keep or sell.

A young prince being handed over to a tutor

Training a prince
All princes were trained to be kings, because no one knew which one would live long enough to take over from his father as king.
A man who did well in the army could get the job of teacher to a young prince.

Mummy of an Egyptian soldier

WINNING FAVOUR

At court it was difficult to get close to the king. But on campaign, a soldier could get the king to notice him by being brave or making a clever suggestion.

This was a good idea because if the king thought a soldier was skilful, he often gave him an important job in the government or at court when they went back home again.

DEATH

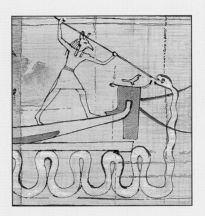

Ready for the afterlife

A successful soldier could afford a tomb and proper

Group of model soldiers

burial equipment. This included a *Book of the Dead* to guide him in the afterlife, models of servants, a fine coffin and all his possessions.

The king's friend

Maiherpri was a great Nubian warrior and friend of King Amenhotep II. He was given the big honour of being buried close to the king's own tomb.

GLOSSARY

A date with "BCE" after it means "before the Common Era" (or "before the birth of Christ", also written as "BC"). A date with "CE" before it means "Common Era" (or "after the birth of Christ", also written as "AD").

Afterlife
The next world, where the ancient Egyptians believed they went when they died. They were buried with things to use in the afterlife.

Alexander the Great (356–323 BCE)
Alexander came from Macedonia (Greece). He took over many lands to make a huge empire.

Archer
Someone who uses a bow to shoot arrows.

Armourer
Someone who made and mended the army's weapons.

Bedouin
Nomadic (wandering) tribespeople who lived in the desert.

Book of the Dead
A book with prayers and spells to help a dead person make the journey to the afterlife.

Bronze
Metal made from copper and tin.

c. (circa)
A Latin word meaning "about". It is used with a date to show that historians are not sure of the exact date.

Campaign
The period of time when an army is fighting an enemy.

Canaanites
People who lived in the land of Canaan (modern Israel, Jordan and Lebanon).

Conscript
Someone forced to join the armed forces.

Conquer
To defeat and take over (e.g. an army or a country).

Cuirass
Armour covering the upper part of the body.

Empire
Group of states, countries or territories that were once independent (not controlled by another country), but now ruled by a single country or person.

Fortified
Strengthened. A building is fortified by building walls and fences to protect it.

Frontier
The edge of a country's territory or land.

Groom
Person who looks after horses.

Hieroglyphics
A type of writing using picture symbols.

Hittites
People from the central area of what is now Turkey. They ruled an empire in the Middle East, and for many years were Egypt's rivals.

Hyksos
Invaders from Canaan, who conquered much of Egypt during the Second

Intermediate Period
(c. 1790–1550 BCE).

Invade/ invasion
To go into another country or land using armed forces.

Medjay
Nubian mercenaries, who became a police force in Egypt.

Mercenary
Professional soldier employed by a foreign state.

Mitanni
The people who, for a time, ruled the land around the upper part of the River Euphrates in modern Iraq. They were wiped out by the Hittites.

Mycenae
Greek city where a fine civilization flourished from c. 1900–1100 BCE.

Patrol
To move around an area to make sure it is safe, or to see what an enemy is doing.

Peleset
A Sea People. After their defeat by Ramesses III

they settled in the land named after them: Palestine. In the Old Testament of the Bible they are called the Philistines.

Pyramid
A huge, triangle-shaped building where dead kings were buried.

Ramesses II
Egyptian king who was famous for the battle of Kadesh, which he claimed to have won on his own. He was a great builder of temples.

Ramesses III
King Ramesses III saved Egypt from invasion by the Sea Peoples.

Scout
Person sent out from an army to discover where the enemy is.

Scribe
Someone who could read and write and made a living by doing so.

Sea Peoples
Peoples thought to be from Mycenaean Greece, its colonies on the west coast of Turkey and the

Aegean Islands. They left their homelands because of famine and unrest. They destroyed many cities and wiped out the Hittite empire. In the end, they were defeated by Ramesses III.

Sherden
One of the Sea Peoples. When some Sherdens were captured by the Egyptians, they became part of the royal bodyguard.

Skirmisher
Soldier carrying few weapons, who fought in a small, short attack.

Standard
Long pole with badges or symbols on it. In battle, it was a gathering point for soldiers. It was carried by a standard-bearer.

Tribute
Taxes paid by defeated peoples to their conquerors.

Tuthmosis III
Egyptian ruler during the New Kingdom. He was perhaps the greatest of all Egypt's warrior kings.

INDEX